SHIFT

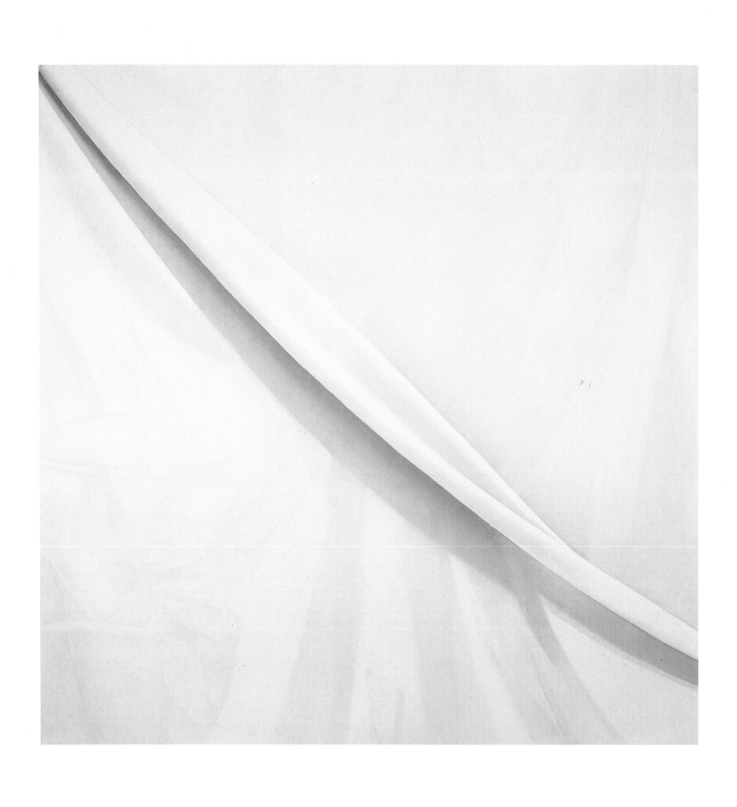

Shift

New Works by Alison Watt

Scottish National Gallery
of Modern Art

Published by the Trustees of the National Galleries
of Scotland for the exhibition *Shift: New Works by Alison
Watt* held at the Scottish National Gallery of Modern Art,
Edinburgh from 18 November 2000 until 7 January 2001

© Trustees of the National Galleries of Scotland 2000
Works by Alison Watt © the artist
ISBN 1 903278 14 7

Photography by Hyjdla Kosaniuk
Designed and typeset in Adobe Garamond by Dalrymple
Printed by BAS Printers, Over Wallop

Cover: detail from *Sabine*, 2000 (catalogue 8)
Frontispiece: *Tuck*, 1999 (catalogue 7)

Foreword

ALISON WATT FIRST CAME to prominence in 1987, when, still a student, she won a commission to paint Her Majesty Queen Elizabeth, The Queen Mother. Watt has since gone from strength to strength, exhibiting regularly here and abroad, and has proved herself to be one of the leading artists to have emerged from Scotland during the last decade.

It is now just over a year since we visited Watt in her Glasgow studio and offered her a solo exhibition at the Scottish National Gallery of Modern Art, making her one of the youngest artists to achieve such recognition. Having begun the *Shift* series in 1997, she has since worked tirelessly to create a remarkable series of new works, which we are delighted to be exhibiting for the first time to the public.

We would like to thank John Calcutt, for his contribution to this catalogue, which has been produced by Janis Adams and Christine Thompson, and designed by Robert Dalrymple. For their help in organising the exhibition we would like to thank Richard and Florence Ingleby, Alice Dewey, Agnes Valencak-Krüger and Judith Lowes. In particular we would like to thank Alison Watt for her dedication to the exhibition.

Shift: New Works by Alison Watt has been generously sponsored by Deutsche Bank, and to their Managing Director and Chief Executive Officer, John Tudor, and their Executive Director, Stephen Connelly, we extend our profound thanks.

TIMOTHY CLIFFORD
Director, National Galleries of Scotland

RICHARD CALVOCORESSI
Keeper, Scottish National Gallery of Modern Art

Sponsor's Foreword

6   DEUTSCHE BANK TODAY employs over 1,000 people in Edinburgh. To celebrate our commitment to the city and Scotland we are delighted to be sponsoring the Scottish National Gallery of Modern Art's exhibition: *Shift: New Works by Alison Watt*.

The bank has a long tradition of supporting modern art, and in particular supporting artists in our many locations throughout the world. Our commitment is based on the conviction that art, as part of our culture and as a major element in our society, should be directly accessible to all.

We are sure that you will enjoy this exhibition of new work by one of Scotland's most exciting contemporary artists.

An Introduction to the Work of Alison Watt

RICHARD CALVOCORESSI

Fig.1 Alison Watt, *Seated Nude,* 1987

THIRTEEN YEARS AGO, Alison Watt, then a twenty-one-year-old postgraduate at Glasgow School of Art, won the John Player Portrait Award at the National Portrait Gallery in London and was commissioned to paint Her Majesty Queen Elizabeth, The Queen Mother. The resulting portrait, iconoclastic yet affectionate, caused a minor scandal. Such notoriety was not entirely welcome to Watt, right at the beginning of her career, but she rode out the storm (no doubt maturing rapidly in the process). And by the time of her first solo exhibition in 1990 she had produced an impressive body of paintings that demanded to be taken seriously: the Queen Mother portrait was clearly not a 'one-off'.

It has been fascinating to follow the development of Watt's imagery over the past decade, from bleached interiors filled with figures (often self-portraits) and witty or symbolic objects; through austere nudes reclining on various types of fabric, meticulously observed (fig.1); to nudes, or anonymous parts of nude bodies, isolated against neutral grounds; and finally to the artist's current absorption in the properties of fabric itself, its power to evoke the human form and human emotions. By her representation initially of highly patterned material, and latterly plain cream material, in various guises from tight tucks to languorous folds, Watt subtly and successfully suggests feelings from high tension to serenity.

It is customary to point to Watt's admiration for Jean-Auguste-Dominique Ingres, whose work she first saw at the National Gallery in London as a child. She rediscovered Ingres on a visit to Paris in 1989, when she spent hours in the Louvre studying his masterpieces at first hand, something she was again able to do in the large exhibition of Ingres's portraits held in London in 1999. The glacial tonality, swelling female shapes and richly patterned materials in her work owe Ingres an obvious debt. It was from this intensive analysis that the *Shift* series of works has evolved, via paintings such as *Sleeper* of 1996 (fig.2), which directly refers to the lush, crumpled fabrics depicted in Ingres's *Odalisque with Slave* of 1842. Even in her most recent 'white paintings' Watt still acknowledges his influence, in titles such as *Sabine* and *Rivière,* which make explicit the human presence implicit in the paintings.

However, there may be a source closer to home for Watt's interest in the classical tradition. Twentieth-century Scottish painting is usually characterised as being concerned more with rich colour and vigorous brushstrokes than with tonal qualities or incisive line. And yet an alternative to the colourist and expressionist traditions (emanating principally from Edinburgh) grew up around the teaching of Maurice Greiffenhagen at the Glasgow School of Art before and after the First World War. Greiffenhangen was an enthusiast for *quattrocento* painting and the Pre-Raphaelites, an enthusiasm he may have imparted to his pupil James Cowie, who in turn taught the two Roberts – Colquhoun and MacBryde – as well as the young Joan Eardley the central importance of drawing.

Asked in 1935 what he considered to be the true function of a painting, James Cowie gave a succinct definition of a kind of art that, in the hands of Alison Watt, shows no sign of losing its power:

> *a picture … must be an idea, a concept built of much that in its total*
> *combination it would never be possible to see and to copy.*

Watt can be considered to belong to this Scottish tradition of painting from the imagination as much as from nature, in a clear precisionist style. She has unwaveringly maintained her independence from the often more explicit approach of her own generation. Instead, her work is based on technical virtuosity in the handling of that most traditional of materials, oil paint, and is characterised by a subtlety which gradually seduces the viewer.

In their emptying of explicit figurative content and rejection of allegory and conceit, Watt's latest 'white paintings' also recall modernist abstraction: the combination of purity and sensuality found in an artist like Lucio Fontana, for example. And as with Fontana – or Yves Klein or Mark Rothko – Watt's new paintings possess a meditative or spiritual quality, their huge scale inviting the viewer's physical participation, his or her willingness to be 'enveloped'. In particular, *Tuck* (frontispiece), painted late last year, can be read as a feminine interpretation of Fontana's violent splitting of the canvas. The single fold which falls elegantly across the entire surface of Watt's painting similarly implies a spatial and spiritual void beyond the edges of her canvas.

This exhibition provides the opportunity to see a remarkable series of new works, shown here for the first time in public. They are carefully considered and meticulously crafted, and are imbued with a sense of maturity and assurance which belies Watt's young age.

8

Fig.2 Alison Watt, *Sleeper,* 1996

Here, There and Everywhere

JOHN CALCUTT

FIRST THERE IS PRESENCE, they said, full and urgent. This is the dream of all painting: to stand alone, complete and independent. Second there is absence, pervasive and melancholy. This is the fate, they said, of all painting: to stand among shadows. Choose. But to paint from both doubt in the given and trust in the unknown is the mark of truly exploratory art. To have and have not: this is the strategy guiding the skill of Alison Watt's work.

Here, in the paintings that form this exhibition, are the residual traces of intensive labour in search of adequate form. Woven into the fabric of these deceptively fast images are entangling threads; threads which, if patiently traced and unpicked, lead through the labyrinth of painting's archive, marking the silent paths of its thought. Painters may begin by facing a white canvas, but they do not face a blank canvas. The undead hordes of near and distant pasts are already at work on that ambushing surface, claiming rights, laying traps, spooking the timid and duping the weak-minded. Jean-Auguste-Dominique Ingres commands the phantoms haunting Watt's endeavour, but she has him under control. Unfortunately for those brave enough to stand their ground, the challenges only increase.

As the first brushstroke heads towards the canvas it is on course to intervene in a mêlée not of its own making. It is bent on destruction – the destruction of some part of that tangled web of innovation and convention known as tradition. A painting-in will also be a painting-out. Immediately it takes up residence on the canvas, however, that same brushstroke becomes the founding moment of another volatile history, that of the painting which it has instigated. Each successive stroke will now open up as many possibilities as it closes down. Two fields of time are now enmeshed, impossible to separate or classify: the past and the future are the closest we can come to naming them. Each retains a gravitational pull equal to the other, this unstable energy expressed in buckle, bulge, implosion and warp. The present has no place here: inside this territory the past is immediately the future, just as the future is always already the past.

Writing strains at its limit when attempting to convey something like this, which is perhaps why the world explained through language is a regimented world of serried units, clipped and arranged to suit the sentence's linear, sequential imperatives. We need paintings like Watt's to remind us that fluidity and complexity, excess and redundancy, contradiction and enigma are everywhere. They are the eruptive geological forces creating that knotted and creased landscape in which the flattened strips cultivated by language are no more than isolated settlements.

Nevertheless, language offers us a place from which to address the world. It offers the illusion that we are at the centre of existence, its hub. The word 'I' is the point at which distance and difference become provisionally assimilated into the self. The pictorial equivalent to the linguistic 'I' is the vanishing point of geometrical perspective, that system of representation in which all receding straight lines converge at a single point on the horizon. Geometrical (or fixed-point) perspective does not simply organise the space within the depicted scene, it also organises the imaginary relation between the viewer and that depicted scene. When the vanishing point is centred in the pictorial field and the pictorial space appears to recede symmetrically and regularly towards it, the fantasising viewer commands and dominates the scene presented before their eyes. The all-knowing 'I' merges with the all-seeing eye. For this illusion of sovereignty to work, however, the viewer must stand centrally before the painted image. A position too far to the left or right will introduce a parallax effect, destroying the experience of spatial continuity between real world and pictorial construction. This disintegration of the optical illusion goes hand in hand with the disintegration of the viewer's own sense of location and controlling presence.

In Watt's paintings of draped and folded fabrics this imminent catastrophe – with its threats of absence and annihilation – is realised. There are no horizons in these images: the sculpted sheets of fabric hang perpendicular, parallel to the canvas surface that supports them. The 'space' of the fabric thus seems to coincide almost exactly with the flat, shallow, lateral space of the pictorial field. There is no deep internal space echoing and extending the viewer's own inhabited space. It is not so much a question of an image being viewed within a pictorial field, as of the image being virtually identical to the pictorial field. The effect of parallax is no longer an issue. As such, Watt's paintings conform to the techniques of trompe l'œil painting (fig.3). This is not merely a technical point, nor is it a solution: it entails further implications. As Norman Bryson remarks:

> *Normally, painting controls the contents of the visual field by means of a sovereign gaze that subordinates everything in the scene to the human observer. But in*

Fig.3 Cornelius Norbertus Gijbrechts, *Trompe L'Oeil: Reversed Canvas,* 1670 (Statens Museum for Kunst, Copenhagen)

trompe l'œil it is as if that gaze has been removed, or had never been present: what we see are objects on their own, not as they are when people are around, but as they really are, left to their own devices.[1]

The viewer is no longer required: the foundations of humanism are thrown into crisis. What if the world had no need of human presence? What if the world regarded itself through its own eyes? What if human values were meaningless for the rest of existence? In this moment Watt's paintings effect the first of a number of epistemological shifts. In the face of these paintings we do not know where we stand: they seem to offer us no meaningful position. Within the system of fixed-point perspective, there are two crucial, interconnected points: the vanishing point and the viewing point. Each validates the other. Here, at a stroke, they have been obliterated.

All is not lost in nihilism, however, because Watt substitutes other possibilities. In place of a point from which to address these works, Watt shifts us towards something more complex, more fascinating: into something that might be called a folded position. If this seems an obscure and difficult concept, it is perhaps no more of an abstraction than that of the point offered by fixed-point perspective. After all, fixed-point perspective is the result of the application of geometric postulates to visual perception (the straight line, for example, is merely a Euclidean wish). The points that pin fixed-point perspective are no more and no less than mathematical constructs – pure conventions, theoretical conveniences. The fold, by contrast, fails to recognise those arbitrary distinctions (the line and the point, the beginning and the end, the past, present and future) by means of which we segregate the world for our own peace of mind. The fold will not support the false oppositions between subject and object, between inside and outside, between mind and body. The fold is nuance, shading, chiaroscuro, continuity.

It would be easy at this point to fall into a trap. What must be avoided is the simplistic and misleading idea that in painting folded fabrics Alison Watt is attempting to literally illustrate the idea of folds. No: the work of folding operates within these images of folds. It is important that we see these paintings, that we bring our bodies to them. Only then do we experience some of the operations of folding produced by them. From a distance, from across the length of a gallery for example, the images appear as just that – images. They parade some of the qualities – sharp, slick, crisp, shiny and seductive – of high-class photography. (This effect also characterises the way they appear when photographically reproduced.) The closer they are approached, however, the more this effect disappears. At some indeterminate distance – an arm's length from the surface, let's say – the illusion of seamless perfection begins to crumble. What had appeared sharp and finely modulated only moments ago now breaks down into an impossible skein of disjointed marks and vague approximations. It is now almost impossible to believe that these same elements could earlier have been mistaken for scintillating sheen and subtle penumbra.

I wrote earlier of trompe l'œil. Those comments must now be modified. The effect of trompe l'œil is certainly present here, but only as a partial condition. Trompe l'œil, it might be said, is staged by Watt as an illusion in its own right, an illusion folded within an illusion, an illusion, moreover, incorporating the conditions of its own disappearance. Once again, this is more than a trick. Watt's paintings appear to employ the techniques of trompe l'œil in order to erase the viewer's fixed viewing position, and thus to suspend the viewer's illusion of mastery. However, once the illusory effects of trompe l'œil itself disappear (as a result of a close-up viewing position), the viewer enters a new situation. At that very moment when trompe l'œil's conceit is exposed, the possibility of a new mode of viewing emerges. The veil of illusion has been lifted, and the painted image now registers and acknowledges the viewing presence of the beholder. The viewer's gaze, as Bryson might say, has been restored. But what does the newly-sighted beholder see? Nothing but confusion. The image has fled, leaving only that incomprehensible scene of disjointed, inarticulate, unexpectedly rough marks. It is a scene that is hard to bear. Having been seduced towards the painted surface, the viewer is now too close. The only option is to retreat, to reinstate that distance which activates the image's disdain. Viewing these paintings, then, is less a matter of occupying a static point than of entering a dynamic fold, a fold in which time, space and self-consciousness constantly wrap around one another in shifting configurations.

In this respect Watt's paintings differ markedly from those by Morris Louis (fig.4), another artist engaged with the interplay between woven fabric, paint and gravity (his paintings often being referred to as 'veils'). Louis would pour acrylic paint directly onto unprimed canvas, allowing it to soak into the woven fibres, the resulting images being dependent upon the gravitational pull of the liquid paint as it gradually seeped through the raw cotton duck canvas. Here there was an absolute identity between image and support (the image not sitting upon the canvas, but stained into it), allowing no room for the parallax effect. Neither were there traces of the physical manufacture of the image, thus no possibility that it might 'break up' on close inspection, its integrity compromised by intimacy. This suppression of 'tactility' and the processes of fabrication ensured that the paintings retained a kind of immaterial transparency, 'accessible to eyesight alone, not to touch.' Nothing was hidden, thus nothing was to be revealed. This resulted, according to Michael Fried, in the collapse of the viewer's experience of space and time: 'It is as though

Fig.4 Morris Louis, *Vav*, 1960
(Tate, London)

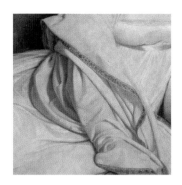

Fig.5 Jean-Auguste-Dominique Ingres, *Madame Rivière*, 1806, detail (Louvre, Paris)

Fig.6 Jean-Auguste-Dominique Ingres, *Madame de Tournon*, 1812, detail (Henry P. McIlhenney Collection, Philadelphia Museum of Art)

one's experience … *has* no duration … because *at every moment the work itself is wholly manifest.*' The eradication of time and space ('of time both passing and to come, *simultaneously approaching and receding*') was the necessary condition, according to Fried, for the experience of 'presentness' – that transcendent state of 'a continuous and perpetual *present*' in which the everyday contingencies of viewing (the shifting relations between work of art and viewer as they are negotiated and re-negotiated within a specific spatial context) were defeated.[2]

One further observation may underline the utter difference between the experiences triggered by Watt's work and those engendered by Louis. The issues of mobility and metamorphosis are central here. I have been writing on the assumption that Watt's paintings are read by the standing observer as representing vertical, perpendicular scenes. It is equally possible, however, to read these draperies not as hanging, but as lying – not as vertical but as horizontal planes. Literally speaking, they could be disheveled beds rather than pendulous shawls. The titles of the paintings only add to such ambivalence. Some – such as *Moitessier, Rivière, Tournon, Sabine* – refer directly to early nineteenth-century portraits of fashionable society women by the French painter Ingres (figs.5 and 6). In such instances, Ingres and his sitters are indexed both linguistically and pictorially (the draperies in Watt's paintings are often transpositions of those in Ingres's). In other cases, however, the titles refer not to individuals but to organic materials (*Milk, Alabaster*) and transitional states (*Suspend, Shift*). In the latter the ambiguity is intensified by an uncertainty as to whether these verbal forms are transitive or intransitive, active or passive, whether they are descriptions or commands. All possibilities remain simultaneously available.

These draperies, these images of bunched, folded and tucked fabrics, enfold us in an enigma. Whatever is present in them also shrouds an absence, an absence we long to bring into presence. They seem to hide something. Writing of trompe l'œil painting, Richard Leppert states:

> *If the deception succeeds, the viewer wants to turn the picture over in order to see what is hidden from sight, the 'real' painting. In effect, the image produces a desire to see, to gain sight of, what it has no intention of satisfying.*[3]

To develop this point, Leppert cites David Summers's claim that all images:

> *involve the transformation of the present. The irreducible and untranslatable significance of images, then, is finally rooted in the intersection and inevitable contradiction between the world's always being present and to us and its seldom being present to us as we desire it to be. Desire for the absent constantly transforms the present.*[4]

We might want to draw back these draperies, tear them away. To find what?

Perhaps the secret is trapped in the figure of the fold. The fold is the very image of fluent transition from visible 'outside' to hidden 'inside'. It is neither pure exteriority nor pure interiority, but a site where they coincide. Its passages unite the seen and the known with dark hidden recesses and dangerous pockets. Perhaps the fold subtly reminds us of that which we wish to forget – that the world is not parcelled into neatly fitting packages of interior space and exterior space, waiting to be connected or disconnected at will. Anxiety may result from this threat of collapsed distinctions – perhaps horror, too. And there is also something unmistakably sexual in play (fig.7). The vagina is perhaps the ultimate embodiment of the fold and its conundrum of absence and presence. It is – as feminists, philosophers, psychoanalysts and misogynists alike agree – the founding site of sexual identity. And the vagina also, as some would argue, prompts a crisis in vision, a crisis re-staged by striptease. As the final garment is removed the sexually inquisitive eye witnesses what it dreads: that there is 'nothing' to be seen. Remember: the myth of Oedipus, so indelibly reinstated by Freud, begins with an enigma and ends in blindness. (Perhaps this is suggested by those rectangular white 'blind spots' in works such as *Tournon* and *Moitessier*.) But the danger here is in reinforcing patriarchal myths, validating men's panic over women's sexual difference. Watt's paintings, as ever, refuse to settle. A sensual knot of damask will mutate into a monstrous cavern as easily as a malevolent eye blossoms into pale flower. Beauty is suffused with a sublime dread, brilliant presence harbours dim absence.

Fig.7 Raphaelle Peale, *Venus Rising from the Sea – A Deception (After the Bath)* c.1822 (Nelson-Atkins Museum of Art, Kansas City)

REFERENCES

1   Norman Bryson, *Looking at the Overlooked: Four Essays on Still-Life Painting*, Harvard University Press, London 1990, p.143.

2   Michael Fried, 'Art and Objecthood', *Artforum*, New York, summer 1967.

3   Richard Leppert, *Art and the Committed Eye*, Westview Press, Oxford 1996, p.25.

4   David Summers, 'Real Metaphor: Towards a Redefinition of the "Conceptual Image"', *Visual Theory: Painting and Interpretation*, (eds) Norman Bryson, Michael Ann Holly and Keith Moxey, HarperCollins, London 1991, p.241.

SABINE, 2000
Oil on canvas, 213.5 × 213.5cm
Catalogue 8 (detail)

TOURNON, 1998–9
Oil on canvas, 213.5 × 213.5cm
Catalogue 4

SUSPEND, 1999
Oil on canvas, 183 x 183cm
Catalogue 6

SHIFT, 2000
Oil on canvas, 213.5 x 213.5cm
Catalogue 10

ROSEBUD, 2000
Oil on canvas, 213.5 × 213.5cm
Catalogue 11

List of Works

1 FOLD, 1997
Oil on canvas, 183 × 152.5cm

2 ALABASTER, 1998
Oil on canvas, 152.5 × 183cm

3 MILK, 1998
Oil on canvas, 152.5 × 183cm

4 TOURNON, 1998–9
Oil on canvas, 213.5 × 213.5cm

5 MOITESSIER, 1999
Oil on canvas, 213.5 × 213.5cm

6 SUSPEND, 1999
Oil on canvas, 183 × 183cm

7 TUCK, 1999
Oil on canvas, 183 × 183cm

8 SABINE, 2000
Oil on canvas, 213.5 × 213.5cm

9 RIVIÈRE, 2000
Oil on canvas, 213.5 × 213.5cm

10 SHIFT, 2000
Oil on canvas, 213.5 × 213.5cm

11 ROSEBUD, 2000
Oil on canvas, 213.5 × 213.5cm

RIVIÈRE, 2000
Oil on canvas, 213.5 × 213.5cm
Catalogue 9 (detail)

Biography

1965   Born, Greenock

1983–7   Glasgow School of Art

1987–8   Glasgow School of Art, Postgraduate Studies

SOLO EXHIBITIONS

1990   *New Paintings,* The Scottish Gallery, London

        New Paintings, Contemporary Art Season, Glasgow Art Gallery & Museum

1993   *New Paintings*, Flowers East, London

1995   *Paintings,* Flowers East, London

1996   *New Paintings,* Belloc Lowndes Fine Art, Chicago

1997   *Monotypes*, Flowers East, London

        Fold, The Fruitmarket Gallery, Edinburgh and tour to Aberdeen Art Gallery & Museum and Leeds Metropolitan University Gallery, 1998

SELECTED GROUP EXHIBITIONS

1986   *British Institute Fund*, Royal Academy, London

1987   *The National Portrait Competition*, National Portrait Gallery, London

1988   *Six Women Artists*, The Scottish Gallery, Edinburgh

1990   *The Compass Contribution – 21 Years of Contemporary Scottish Art*, The Tramway, Glasgow

1991   *Nudes*, Flowers East at Watermans Art Centre, Middlesex

1992   *As I see Myself: Artists in their Work*, Plymouth City Museum & Art Gallery

1993   *New Figurative Painting*, Salander-O'Reilly Galleries with Fred Hoffman, Los Angeles

1995   *An American Passion*, McLellan Galleries, Glasgow, and tour to Royal College of Art, London and Yale Center for British Art, New Haven, Connecticut

        The Continuing Tradition: 75 Years of Painting, Glasgow School of Art

1996   *Making a Mark: Figure*, Mall Galleries, London

        The Power of Images, Martin Gropius Bau, Berlin

        Four British Painters, John McEnroe Gallery, New York

1996 *Bad Blood*, Glasgow Print Studio (exhibitor and curator)

British Painting, Mendenhall Gallery, Pasadena

1997 *Treasures for Everyone*, National Art Collections Fund, Christie's, London

From the Interior – Female Perspectives on Figuration, Ferens Art Gallery, Hull and tour to Stanley Picker Gallery, Kingston University and tour in China, 1999

Von Kopf Bis Fuss, Ursula Buckle Stiftung, Kraichtal

Body Politic, Wolverhampton Art Gallery

10th Anniversary Portfolio, The Freud Museum, London

1998 *Londres, Glasgow, Edimbourg*, Galerie Rachlin LeMarie, Paris

1999 *The Human Figure in Contemporary Art*, Galerie de Bellefeuille, Montreal

AWARDS

1986 British Institution Fund: First Prize for Painting, Royal Academy, London

Glasgow Competition: First Prize, Glasgow School of Art

1987 The John Player Portrait Award, National Portrait Gallery, London

Armour Prize for Still Life Painting, Glasgow School of Art

1989 The Elizabeth Greenshields Foundation Award, Montreal

The Morrison Scottish Portrait Award: Special Commendation, Royal Scottish Academy, Edinburgh

1993 The City of Glasgow Lord Provost Prize

1996 Scottish Arts Council: Individual Artist's Award

COLLECTIONS

Aberdeen Art Gallery

British Broadcasting Corporation

Christie's Corporate Art Collection

Ferens Art Gallery, Hull

The Fleming-Wyfold Art Foundation

The Freud Museum, London

Glasgow Art Gallery & Museum

McMaster University Art Gallery, Ontario

National Portrait Gallery, London

National Westminster Bank, London

MOITESSIER, 1999
Oil on canvas, 213.5 × 213.5cm
Catalogue 5

My thanks are due to David Brown, John
Calcutt, Keith Hartley, Richard Calvocoressi,
Richard and Florence Ingleby, James and Nancy
Watt and especially Ruaridh Nicoll.

ALISON WATT